HOWGILLS AND LIMESTONE TRAIL

HOWGILLS AND LIMESTONE TRAIL

A new walk in the footsteps
of Alfred Wainwright

David & Heather Pitt

F

FRANCES LINCOLN LIMITED
PUBLISHERS

For
James Trevelyan
and
Hilary Grayson

The summit of The Calf, Howgill Fells

Dear friends
in whose company
we enjoyed many walks
and lovely holidays

Frances Lincoln Ltd
Aurum Publishing Group
74–77 White Lion Street
London N1 9PF
www.franceslincoln.com

Howgills and Limestone Trail
Text copyright © David & Heather Pitt 2013
Foreword copyright © W.R. Mitchell 2013
Illustrations copyright © Colin Bywater 2013
Maps and vignettes copyright © Ron Scholes 2013

First Frances Lincoln edition 2013

A catalogue record for this book is available from
the British Library.

ISBN 978-0-7112-3444-4

Printed and bound in China

CONTENTS

ACKNOWLEDGMENTS

The primary acknowledgement is, unsurprisingly, to Alfred Wainwright himself, whose writings, pictorial guides to the Howgill Fells and Limestone Country and sketchbooks have provided virtually all the background material. His love of the area, its history and people shine out from their pages. Chief among his writings is *Westmorland Heritage*, the book that he produced at the time of the demise of Westmorland as a county in its own right and its absorption into the new county of Cumbria. This has, in addition to factual information about places along the route, provided a rich vein of sketches for the guide.

Then, of course, come Ron Scholes and Colin Bywater, whose maps, vignettes and drawings bring this book to life. They are followed by our friends Derek and Alison Cockell (not forgetting Beattie their Bedlington terrier) who accompanied us during the final test walking. Also to James and Felicity Trevelyan of Bridge End, Barbon who provided hospitality for all the walkers involved while in their area.

Finally there has been the memory for David, as we walked along that section of the route in the Lune valley shared with the Dales Way, of his 1979 Dales Way walk with his father, Harry Pitt. Then a mere seventy-seven-year-old, he was undertaking a long-distance walk for the first time and enjoyed every minute and stride of it.

FOREWORD

As a personal friend of Alfred Wainwright, I realised he had a fondness for the area outlined in this book, which has been devised, in the style of AW, by some of his greatest fans. The area concerned is handy – but well out of sight of Kendal, where AW lived and worked and from where he set out on his lone expeditions. And here, twixt the Silurian rocks of the Lakes and the Carboniferous rocks of the Dales, were some of his favourite landscapes.

Normally, this is a quiet countryside. A walker might enjoy spells of solitude. Paths have not been badly eroded. In the nesting season, curlews can make themselves heard – except when a train is clattering through the steep-sided Lune Gap, a sight that will appeal to railway fans. The route makes wide detours from the Lunesdale road, away from the whoosh of motor traffic, into an old-time countryside. The gently rounded Howgill Fells do not over-tax the lungs of the rambler.

Wainwright loved to stand by tumbling water. A walker, with the eastern side of the Howgills in view, glimpses a short valley, at the head of which is the spectacular Cautley Spout, where water descends a steep eastern flank of the smooth fells in a series of leaps totalling 700 feet. On the Trail are the Ingleton Waterfalls, which include the majesty of Thornton Force. It had a strong appeal to Wainwright during his Pennine Journey of 1938.

Walkers on the Howgills and Limestone Trail begin their adventures in Kirkby Stephen and end them at Settle, these being market towns that have kept their old-style character. After crossing flat-topped Ingleborough, on the Limestone Trail, you descend into North Ribblesdale. Arrange to stop for a snack where the Ribble at Stainforth is spanned by a packhorse-type bridge. As you ponder on your walk, let an Elgarian strain pass through your mind – Elgar loved this spot and had a photograph of it in his home.

W.R. Mitchell

HOWGILLS and LIMESTONE TRAIL

Smardale Gill Viaduct

View to Fell Head

HOWGILL FELLS

Kirkby Stephen

Ravenstonedale

Cautley

Sedbergh

Ease Gill Kirk

Barbon

Summit of Penyghent

INGLEBOROUGH

PENYGHENT

Pecca Twin Falls

Ingleton

Horton in Ribblesdale

R5

Settle

St. Leonard's Church, Chapel-le-Dale

Erratic boulder, Upper Winskill

INTRODUCTION

First and foremost, this pictorial guide is a tribute to Alfred Wainwright (AW), who loved the Howgill Fells and the limestone area around the Three Peaks. He was so captivated by the whole area close to his home in Kendal that he wrote a pair of slim pictorial guides to two distinct areas — *Walks in Limestone Country*, published in 1970, and *Walks on the Howgill Fells*, published in 1972. Both these guidebooks, which are currently being updated, are still in print and should be considered desirable companions to this guide.

They were essential reading in the 1990s when we were devising our version of AW's 1938 Pennine Journey, and part of that route was based on them. It was during the latter stages of the Pennine Journey project to revise our 1998 route that we became increasingly fascinated by the area — an area that we had enjoyed walking in from time to time, using our pictorial guides, over the preceding twenty-five years. We wondered if it might be possible, using material from AW's guides, to create a long-distance footpath from Kirkby Stephen to Settle throughout this area of Cumbria and North Yorkshire — with a short diversion into Lancashire. Subsequently we realised that walkers could utilise the Pennine Journey route in reverse from Settle to create a circular walk of around 134 miles.

At the end of the Pennine Journey project, Ron Scholes, who drew the route maps for the guidebook, asked, probably tongue in cheek 'What's next?' We mentioned, hesitatingly, our idea and got an immediate enthusiastic response. We suppose it should have been anticipated as, during the time we had got to know Ron, we appreciated that he (like AW, whom he knew well) had for a long time had a great love of the whole area, and of the Howgill Fells in particular.

A route was devised, sent to Ron for his consideration and, after a few minor revisions, mainly during the route's preliminary test walking, agreed. He then made several trips to the area to walk the route, making his notes for the route maps as he went. Colin Bywater, who had done the excellent black and white drawings for the Pennine Journey pictorial guide was happy to rejoin the team responsible for that production – this time though with a much bigger role. For that book it was only possible for eighteen of the thirty-six drawings to be re-interpretations of sketches done by AW, but for this guidebook, because of the wealth of material from *Westmorland Heritage*, nearly all the drawings are re-interpretations.

Finally one theme runs throughout the entire route: railways 'ancient and modern'. Kirkby Stephen, in the heyday of trains, had two lines running close to the town. The 'ancient' one is the Stainmore railway, which carried coal from the Durham coalfields to the steel industries of Barrow and the West Coast of Cumberland for just over a hundred years. Very close to Kirkby Stephen are some wonderful viaducts and the route passes over the finest of them: Smardalegill. The 'modern' one is the Settle–Carlisle railway line, which was saved from closure in 1986 and Settle station is the end of the trail. Between Kirkby Stephen and Settle the trail passes close to the trackbed of the disused Ingleton–Tebay railway, which for a large part of its route follows the River Lune and passes through Barbon and Sedbergh. This section also possesses some wonderful viaducts which have been preserved. For the long-distance footpath walker who has an interest in railways then the Howgills and Limestone Trail is a 'must'.

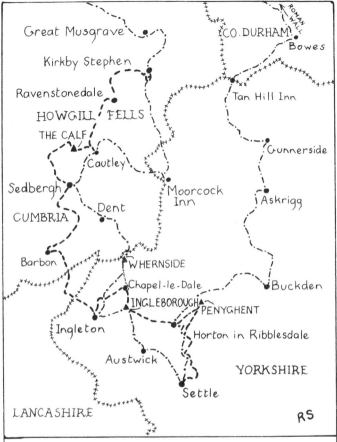

THE HOWGILLS AND LIMESTONE TRAIL
IN RELATION TO THE SOUTHERN
SECTION OF THE PENNINE JOURNEY

Howgills and Limestone Trail   — — — — —

Pennine Journey   — · — · —   Co. Boundary   + + + + + +

KEY–SIGN REFERENCES
(signs and abbreviations used in the maps)

Road ═══

Track ═════

Walking routes

MAIN ROUTE: – – – – –

OTHER ROUTES – – – – – –

Bridge —)(—

Church +

Building

Woods

    conifer

    deciduous

Crag

Boulders

Limestone pavement

Ancient earthwork

Map scale: 2½ inches = 1mile

North is top of the page

Railway

River, Stream

Wall ∞∞∞∞∞∞∞

Broken wall ∘ ∘ ∘ ∘ ∘

Fence +++++++++

Hedge

Footbridge FB

Way marker WM

Cattle grid CG

Former railway

Contours (at 100′ intervals)

    800
    900

Summit ●

Ordnance Survey column

▲ with O.S number

(triangulation point)

Miles (from starting point), and direction of route.

㉖ ➤ – – –

PW – Pennine Way

RS

DAY ONE

Kirkby Stephen to Ravenstonedale

Distance	8½ miles
Highest Point	855 feet
Height Ascended	1,244 feet
Going	Easy
Map	O.S. Explorer OL19

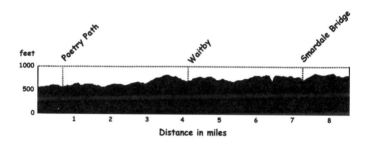

Kirkby Stephen rivals Appleby as the premier market town of the Eden Valley and is an excellent centre for exploring the charms of the valley as well as the adjacent Yorkshire Dales and the nearby Howgill Fells. It was granted a market charter in 1353 by Edward III and a further one in 1605 by James I on the application of the Earl of Cumberland, Lord of Kirkby Manor. The derivation of the town's name is uncertain; Kirkby is of Norse origin meaning a settlement with a church and there are several theories why Stephen came to be associated. The church, known locally as the 'Cathedral of the Dales' is an elegant twelfth-century one within which is the ninth-century Loki Stone with its carving of the Norse god. The church is the third one on the site following a Norman one, which replaced a Saxon one and its principal entrance is the ornate sandstone colonnaded Cloisters, erected in 1810. It was here that the Monday butter market was held. The town does not feature in the Domesday Book as at that time this part of Cumberland and Westmorland was, by conquest, part of the Kingdom of Strathclyde.

Entrance to St Stephen's Church

The trail starts at the entrance to St Stephen's Church in the market square – a spot where many walkers start the stage of Alfred Wainwright's Coast to Coast Walk over Nine Standards Rigg to Keld, and where others leave on their stage of the Pennine Journey down the Eden Valley to Garsdale Head. Soon the Poetry Path is encountered – its twelve short poems carved on blocks of stone describe a year in the life of a hill farmer and are situated at intervals on a circular path. A leaflet describing the Poetry Path in full can be purchased from the Tourist Information Centre in Kirkby Stephen. This, like the Eden Benchmarks – ten sculptures placed closed to the Eden between its source in Mallerstang and where it enters the sea at the Solway Firth

November Poetry Stone

— is another East Cumbria Countryside Project which Dick Capel helped to establish. Part of the way along the Poetry Path the trail passes the Benchmark named 'Passage'.

The route of the Coast to Coast Walk is joined as it passes around the prehistoric earthworks of Croglam Castle and Kirkby Stephen East station on the disused Darlington–Tebay line. Soon another section of this line is met: one that has been transformed by the Cumbria Wildlife Trust into Smardalegill National Nature Reserve, which is a 3½-mile section on either side of the magnificent Smardalegill Viaduct, now under the stewardship of the Northern Viaducts Trust. Again, the Coast to Coast Walk is met on its approach to Smardale Bridge but it is left there as the trail makes its way across the remains of what was a walled deer park created by the first Lord Wharton, who purchased the land following the Dissolution of the Monasteries in the mid-sixteenth century. Ravenstonedale, with its two old hostelries, the Black Swan Hotel and the Kings Head, is soon reached after crossing the A685.

Route Description

From the colonnaded entrance to the church, take the walled lane (Stone Shot) signed to the River Eden and Frank's Bridge. Very soon, after a bend, take some steps on the left which lead to Mellbecks. The route goes right here, but a short diversion for a few yards leads to Frank's Bridge over the River Eden. The Coast to Coast Walk passes over the bridge on its way out of Kirkby Stephen to Nine Standards Rigg and Keld; and the Pennine Journey uses the bridge on its way into and out of Kirkby Stephen.

Frank's Bridge, Kirkby Stephen

Return to the steps and head up Mellbecks – a quiet backwater which parallels Kirkby Stephen's main street. This emerges onto the Nateby road to the left of the imposing Temperance Hall, with its painted lady in the niche above the front door. Turn left and follow the road that rises after passing the school. One hundred yards after the brow of the hill, take a footpath on the left (FP to Stenkrith and BW to Hartley and Nateby), which marks the start of the Poetry Path. This path, Bolam Lane, leads down to the River Eden.

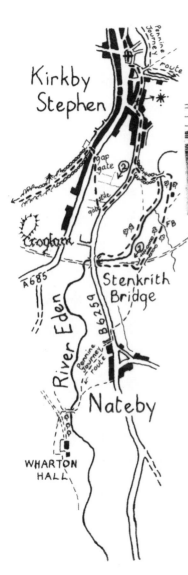

Kirkby Stephen

Croglam

River Eden

A685

B6259

Stenkrith Bridge

map gate

little gate

FB

Pennine Journey route

Nateby

WHARTON HALL

* FACADE
TEMPERANCE HALL 1865
Kirkby Stephen

At a gate, ignore the public footpath sign and continue down the lane. The poem for January is carved on a stone on the right where the path meets the Eden at a kissing gate and a footbridge. Cross the bridge (BW & FP: Pod Gill & Ewbank Scar) to arrive soon at February's poem inscribed on blocks of stone, close to a stone barn. After a further 150 yards at a gate turn right onto a sunken path, which has been used for hundreds of years and could have been the road linking Kirkby Stephen and Nateby – here the Pennine Journey is joined. The path drops down to a footbridge over a stream where March's stone can be seen on the left. The path, now between steep banks, ascends gently and soon passes the April stone incorporated into the wall on the right. May's poem is also built into a dry stone wall on the left before the path crosses a bridge over a disused railway which was built between 1857 and 1860 primarily to take coal from the coalfields of Durham to the shipyards at Barrow-in-Furness. Almost immediately, June's stone is on the right before a gate which is taken onto the disused railway line. It is here that the Pennine Journey is left as it continues to Nateby. Turn left along the trackbed, which is owned and managed as a nature reserve by the Northern Viaduct Trust. The stones for July, August and September now follow in quick succession on both sides of the footpath. Ahead is the road bridge over this former trackbed and here turn right onto a Millennium Bridge over the River Eden. Pause to look at the river and wonder at the time taken to carve the channels in the river bed. After crossing the river, take a thin track on the right just past a green metal seat and, on reaching a stony track, turn right towards the river. Soon the path passes the two prone stones bearing the October poem. Take a path on the right just before another green metal seat, which leads through trees to the Eden Benchmark 'Passage', mentioned earlier. Return to the path, turn right and soon on the left is the November poem, inscribed on two vertical slabs of stone set at right angles to each other. Go over the stile, take the gently climbing path and follow the river to a kissing gate. Stay close to the river bank to arrive at the final

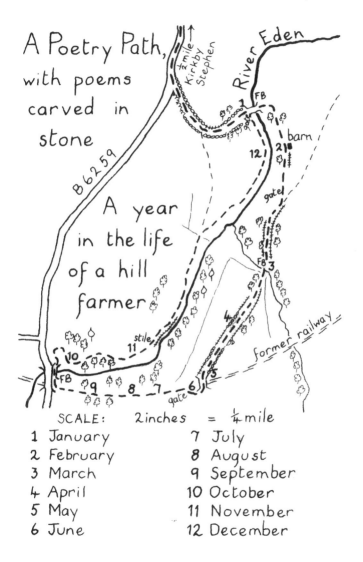

A Poetry Path, with poems carved in stone

½ mile Kirkby Stephen ↑

River Eden

B6259

A year in the life of a hill farmer

FB

barn

gate

stile

former railway

gate

SCALE: 2 inches = ¼ mile

1 January
2 February
3 March
4 April
5 May
6 June
7 July
8 August
9 September
10 October
11 November
12 December

poetry stones with the footbridge, crossed at the start of the Poetry Path, immediately ahead.

Go back up Bolam Lane to the Nateby road, turn left and after approximately 200 yards take a path on the right (FP South Road) at a kissing gate. After passing through the gate and gap stile, head diagonally towards and through trees, passing behind the rear of a line of houses to reach a gate beyond the last one. This leads onto South Road, turn right and after a few yards take the first entry on the left to reach the back lane at a play area.

This is the route of the Coast to Coast Walk into Kirkby Stephen but here turn left. This soon becomes a stony track and then is metalled but where it bends left, go straight ahead on a stony track which is the drive to Greenriggs Farm. To the left on the high ground is the earthwork of Croglam Castle. On the approach to the farm, across the meadow to the left, are sidings of what was Kirkby Stephen East station. The footpath has been diverted around the farm so take the alternative route on the right through a gate and head around the facing barn. Follow the waymarks through two gates then turn right through a further gate to take the underpass of the disused railway line, pausing to look back at notices on the barn wall for the benefit of Coast to Coast walkers. Go through a gate on the right heading up the field with a wall on the left to a stile in the field corner. Go slightly right to enter a dry gully and where this widens a marker post shows the way ahead.

The path now heads to an underpass in the Settle–Carlisle railway crossing ancient settlements just before reaching it. Here the Coast to Coast Walk continues through the underpass but this route heads right, paralleling the railway, to a gate. The path rises and at the top good views can be had of the Pennines. Head diagonally right, skirting a gully, to reach the road at another gate in the wall corner. Turn right down the lane and left at the next junction towards Waitby, through which AW passed on his 1938 Pennine Journey. After passing a farmhouse with a 1641 date stone, take the Smardale road to the left at the crossroads.

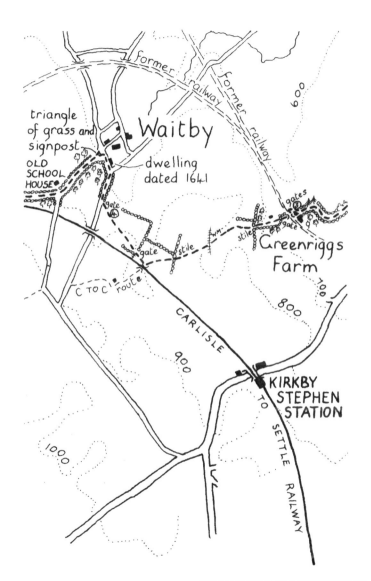

triangle
of grass and
signpost

OLD
SCHOOL
HOUSE

former railway

former railway

600

Waitby

dwelling
dated 1641

gates

gate

stile

gate

stile

C TO C route

WM

Greenriggs
Farm

700

CARLISLE

800

900

KIRKBY
STEPHEN
STATION

TO

SETTLE RAILWAY

1000

CARLISLE TO SETTLE

Old Smardale Station, now a private residence with a lovely garden

former railway

RAILWAY

⑤
½ mile
WAITBY →

HALL

Scandal Beck

⑥
NATIONAL
NATURE
RESERVE

Quarry

RS

SMARDALEGILL
VIADUCT

Smardale Fell

Soon what was Waitby school is reached — now a private dwelling with the bell and housing still retained. Continue on past a lane that joins from the left and head down the hill to Smardale. Across the fields to the left can be seen the farm complex of Smardale Hall.

Smardale Hall

At the next junction, bear right to cross over the bridge of the disused railway line. This overlooks the lovely house and gardens of the former Smardale station. Follow the road left and after a few yards turn left towards Smardale Hall. A stony track leads from a gate on the right to a prominent board for the Smardalegill National Nature Reserve and the bed of the old railway track which is followed for just over 2 miles. The route passes through the nature reserve, initially contouring the heavily wooded, steep-sided valley of Scandal Beck. On this section in late summer look out for the Scotch Argus butterfly – this is only one of two places in England where it can be seen. Just as the valley starts to open out, with views of the Howgill Fells ahead, the route passes over the magnificent Smardalegill Viaduct, now under the stewardship of the

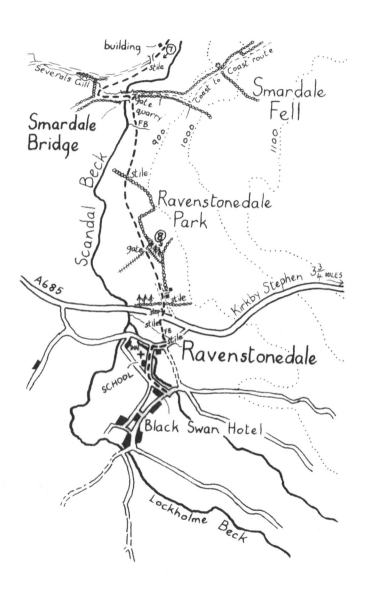

building

(7)

stile

Severals Gill

Coast to Coast route

Smardale Fell

gate

quarry

FB

Smardale
Bridge

900

1000

1100

stile

Scandal Beck

Ravenstonedale
Park

(8)

gate

A685

Kirkby Stephen 3¾ MILES →

stile

step

stile

FB

stile

Ravenstonedale

INN

✝

SCHOOL

Black Swan Hotel

Lockholme Beck

Smardale Bridge

Northern Viaducts Trust. Soon a huge double limekiln is reached, built to take advantage of the Darlington–Tebay railway line, which supplied lime to steelworks at Barrow and Darlington. After passing two derelict railway cottages, the path leaves the old railway track at a bridge where it joins the Coast to Coast Walk, dropping down to Smardale Bridge.

Immediately over the beck, take a path through a gate on the right (FP Ravenstonedale) which initially stays close to sandstone outcrops, cross a small wooden footbridge then head gently uphill away from the river towards a gate and stile in the facing wall. Bear left uphill across the next field towards the right hand corner of a copse of trees and a barn beyond, which soon come into view. Once through the gate, head towards the barn to pick up a track which passes an older barn and where the track turns left take a facing stile and drop down some steps through the trees to reach the A685. Cross this busy road with care and take the facing steps and a stile. Cross the field and at the road turn right to enter the village of Ravenstondale, then turn left to pass the church and school and reach the Black Swan Hotel, which interestingly now incorporates the village store.

DAY TWO

Ravenstonedale to Cautley

Distance	9½ miles
Highest Point	1,422 feet
Height Ascended	1,299 feet
Going	Easy
Map	O.S. Explorer OL19

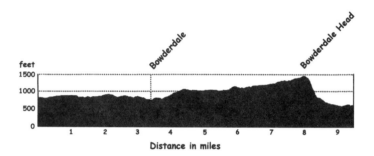

Ravenstonedale is situated in a wooded valley nestling at the foot of the Howgill Fells and is surrounded by an open landscape. This open fell landscape, in Roman times, had many small scattered farmsteads and settlements like the ones passed on the trail on the approach to Waitby. Other settlements nearby have shown evidence of Bronze Age occupation.

The village itself is widespread with, at the heart of its open centre, the parish church of St Oswald's and the village school close to Scandal Beck. The church is early eighteenth century but built on a much earlier foundation which is probably Saxon, as part of a Saxon cross stands close to its porch. It has an interesting interior, in the collegiate style, with rows of pews facing a central aisle. On the north side are the excavated ruins of a Gilbertine Abbey built around AD 1200. The Gilbertines, named

St Oswald's Church, Ravenstonedale

after St Gilbert, who reputedly lived to be over 100 years old, were the only English Monastic Order and the Dissolution of the Monasteries meant its demise.

Not surprisingly there are several factors that are common to places along the Howgills and Limestone Trail and the Pennine Journey. Lead was mined in the area in the 1820s and 1830s by the ubiquitous London Lead Company and knitting was also a well established means of supplementing low incomes. Lord Brougham, at an election meeting at the Black Swan in 1826 is said to have quipped 'This parish ought to be called Knitting Dale'.

The major part of this stage's route is very straightforward once the trail, which skirts the Howgill Fells, has passed through the nurseries at Weasdale and arrives at Bowderdale Foot with its lovely old farmhouse. A delightful, long lonely walk up Bowderdale follows, leading to the heart of the Howgills with the slopes of Randygill Top (2,047 feet) and then Yarlside (2,097

Cautley Spout

feet) dominating the view eastwards. The path climbs very gradually to Bowderdale Head and it is here that the impressive cliffs of Cautley Crag suddenly come into view. Soon, on the descent down to Cautley, more and more of the falls of Cautley Spout are revealed and after passing through an area of an early settlement the River Rawthey is crossed by the Cross Keys Inn, Cautley. This was a favourite place for sustenance for Alfred Wainwright while he was walking in the area prior to writing his *Walks on the Howgill Fells*. The book contains a sketch by him of the inn with a 'Ham and Eggs' sign on the roadside verge prominent in the foreground – still there forty years later.

Route Description

From the Black Swan Hotel go past the Old Vicarage on the left and at the fork by the school go left passing firstly the school on the right and then the church. The road bends to the right past the King's Head and on meeting the road turn left. Continue along this quiet road which was formerly the main road until the now

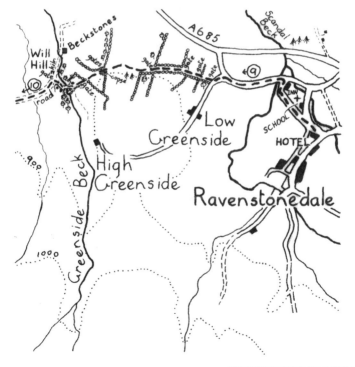

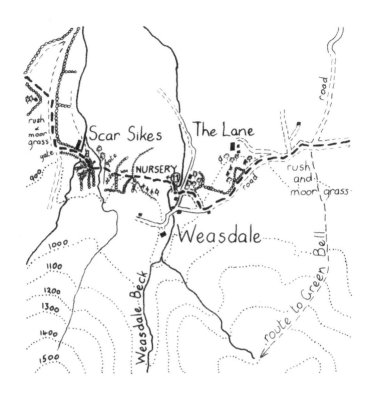

audible A685, which bypasses Ravenstonedale, was built on the trackbed of the old South Durham & Lancashire Union railway line. Ignore the first footpath on the left hand side signed to Low Greenside and almost immediately after take the lane on the left signed Greenside ¼ mile. After 100 yards take a footpath on the right (BW Will Hill) through the gate and pass through two fields keeping close to the wall on the left to enter a green lane which terminates at a gate. The path stays by the left hand wall heading for a clump of trees. In the trees on the left a gate leads to another short track between a barbed wire fence and limestone wall then leads into a large meadow. Cross this to a gate beneath a large sycamore tree. From here the path continues downhill on an old track, beside a newly built wall on the right, to a barn. After crossing a bridge over Greenside Beck the path comes to a gate passing a farmhouse on the left to reach a metalled road. Turn left with the Howgills Fells ahead.

The lane reaches another lane: turn left signed to Weasdale Nurseries. At a fork, keep left following the directions to Weasdale Nurseries and stay on the road. After passing a ruined farmhouse on the left take a green track on the right down under the power cables towards the trees. This path emerges onto a track by the entrance to Weasdale Nurseries; turn left then take the path through a wicket gate in the wall on the right (FP Browfoot). Head down through a small stand of trees and cross a metal bridge which has been placed over an old stone bridge over Weasdale Beck. The path goes through a gate in a deer fence to pass through part of the

Bowderdale Foot

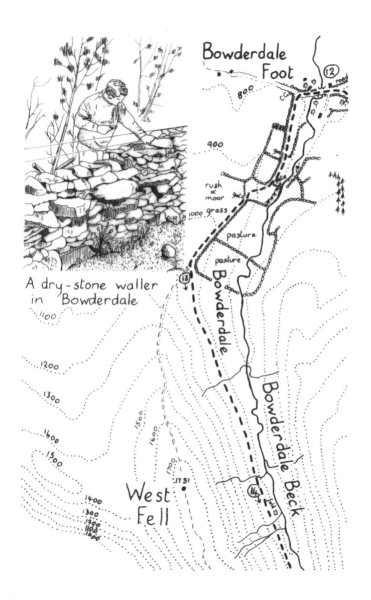

Bowderdale
Foot

road

rush
&
moor

1000 grass

pasture

pasture

Bowderdale

Bowderdale Beck

A dry-stone waller
in Bowderdale

West
Fell

1751

nurseries. Follow the directional signs through here until a gate in the deer fence is seen ahead. Here head diagonally left on a faint track through a partially deforested area which leads to a wicket gate in the deer fence. Once through, head right where a marker post indicates the way ahead to a ladder stile in the facing wall with Scar Sikes farm ahead across the meadow. Pass to the left of the farmhouse, through the farmyard and take the farm drive ahead to reach and turn right on a metalled lane. This farm drive is a permissive path by kind permission of the farmer. Opposite a stone barn by four mature trees head off left on a faint track.

This becomes rutted as it passes the barn then becomes stony as it leads down to the road in Bowderdale. Cross the attractive double arched bridge over Bowderdale Beck with the old farmhouse of Bowderdale Foot shyly hidden amongst the trees ahead.

Continue past Bowderdale Foot and take a bridleway on the left (SP Bowderdale) just before the cattle grid – this is the beginning of a very straightforward section of today's walk. After

Bowderdale

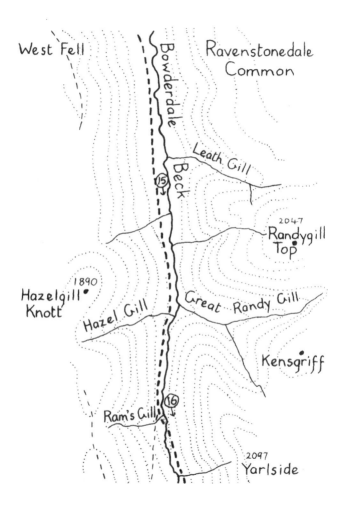

West Fell

Ravenstonedale
Common

Bowderdale Beck

Leath Gill

15

2047
Randygill
Top

1890
Hazelgill
Knott

Hazel Gill

Great Randy Gill

Kensgriff

16

Ram's Gill

2097
Yarlside

passing through two gates bear right to a third where the path enters open moorland with a wall on the left. Straight away good vistas of the Howgill Fells open up. As the wall drops away to the beck the path continues ahead to meet the beck and follows it for about two miles.

It then begins to climb gently, still following the beck, and after another mile when it crosses Ram's Gill, the main track, which heads upwards in a grooved track for The Calf, is left. Drop

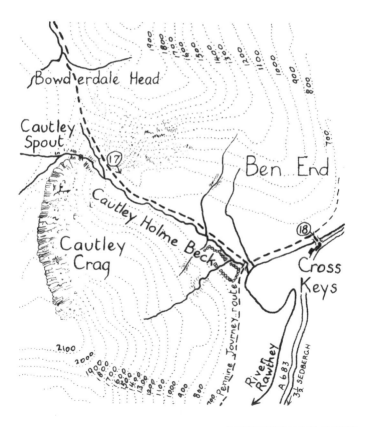

Cautley Crags

down towards the beck and on the hillside opposite a faint track can be seen through the grass heading for Bowderdale Head. On the approach to the head of Bowderdale the impressive mile long line of Cautley Crag comes into view and soon afterwards can be seen the upper falls of Cautley Spout.

Dropping down, more of the falls come into view. From the point at which the route will tomorrow head off to climb by the side of the falls to the top of The Calf, the major fall is very much in evidence. Eventually the path becomes wider as it reaches the valley bottom and follows close to the river. A bridge crossing Cautley Holme Beck comes into view and it is over this bridge that the Pennine Journey makes its way to Sedbergh but this walk passes by the bridge, continuing straight on to the next footbridge over the Rawthey to reach the Cross Keys Inn and the end of this stage.

DAY THREE

Cautley to Sedbergh

Distance   11¾ miles
Highest Point   2,207 feet
Height Ascended   2,940 feet
Going   Strenuous with one steep climb
Map   O.S. Explorer OL19

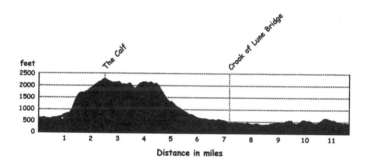

The history of the Cross Keys Inn, Cautley, is an interesting one with its origins going back to the mid-sixteenth century based on dated oak panelling in its library. Records from 1614 have it as a farmhouse known as High Haygarth which was extended about a century later. Coincidentally, given its location in the Rawthey valley close to the summit of The Calf the highest summit in the Howgill Fells, over the door are the initials of John and Agnes Howgill who owned it at the time of its extension. When the turnpike road to Sedbergh was built it became an inn and was further extended during the early nineteenth century.

As an inn it has a curious history, being a temperance hotel since 1902 when a drunken local resident who had fallen into the River Rawthey was saved by the landlord who died in the attempt. The family of the survivor bought the inn and, after immediately relinquishing the liquor licence, sold it to the Bunney family. On the death of Adelaide Bunney in 1947, the Cross Keys was left to the National Trust and a proviso in her will stated that it should never again sell alcohol.

Cross Keys Inn, Cautley

The Cross Keys Inn has also a very strong Quaker connection having been owned in 1652 by Gervase Benson, a local landowner and former colonel in Cromwell's army, who was one of a group of local people who were dissatisfied by current religious practice. It is highly likely that he listened to a speech given by George Fox from a crag on the nearby Firbank Fell (now known as Fox's Pulpit) in 1652 attended by over 1,000 people and many believe that the formation of the Quaker movement arose from this event. The connection continues to this day as the current tenant, Alan Clowes, is a practising Quaker. Well worth a visit to anyone with time to spare in the area is the Quaker Tapestry, a series of panels, which can be viewed at the Friends Meeting House in Kendal. These illustrate the real contribution made to the industry and commerce of Great Britain, and further

Morrisons

since 1889

WM Morrison Supermarkets PLC BD3 7DL

Coalville - 01530 814666

Manager : Barry Baines

VAT No.343475355

QTY DESCRIPTION	PRICE	AMOUNT
1 M BRIT S SKIM MILK	£1.15	£1.15 F
1 AMBI PUR REFILL	£3.00	£3.00 A
BALANCE DUE		£4.15
Cash		£5.00
CHANGE		£0.85
Number of items:		2

****

Morrisons More

Your Balance as of yesterday: 1045

Total More Points earned today:

More Points   20

For more details visit www.morrisons.com/more

****

Your Survey Entry No:620000540160190

22/12/2018 18:56:10 00054 010 0190 0052

THANK YOU FOR SHOPPING
AT MORRISONS

afield, by Quakers and the individual tapestries contain thoughts and ideas with which no thinking person could disagree.

At the front of *Walks on the Howgill Fells* AW uses a quotation from William Blake which appears carved on a lintel above a door within the inn and which reads:

> Great things are done when men and mountains meet.
> These are not done by jostling in the street.

This stage completes the traverse of the Howgill Fells that began yesterday. It starts by retracing the final mile back to where the path leaves to start the climb past the magnificent Cautley Spout – England's highest waterfall above ground. The broken cascade of falls tumbles a total of 650 feet down a cliff face at the head of a valley that comes down from The Calf. After admiring the succession of waterfalls the path arrives at The Calf (2,200 feet) – the highest point of the Howgill Fells – from where there is a wonderful panoramic view.

Summit of The Calf

Then follows a 2-mile ridge walk to Fell Head (2,045 feet) before a descent into the Lune valley where the River Lune is met at the very narrow Crook of Lune Bridge. Marks on the bridge parapets bear witness to the need for motorists to cross with care. It is here that the route meets that of the Dales Way, an 80-mile long-distance footpath devised in 1970 by Colin Speakman between Ilkley and Windermere. The path follows the Lune downstream for nearly 3 miles passing below Firbank Fell before going across country to Sedbergh where the stage ends at St Andrew's Church built around 1500.

Route Description

Return to Cautley Spout and on approaching the waterfalls take the path on the left which soon begins to ascend on a pitched path close to the falls. At one point the pitched path becomes a track as it contours around a hillside and then continues as a pitched path to the top of the falls. At the head of the falls continue on the track to the right of the beck which eventually arrives at a substantial and well maintained sheepfold.

Sheepfold by Red Gill Beck

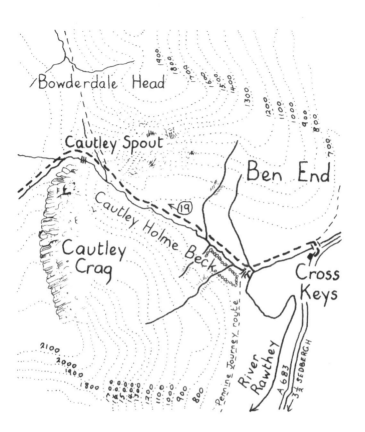

Just beyond, two becks converge. Here take the track to the right hand side of the beck on the right. Soon, at a col, a broad track is reached and at the same point a bridleway comes in from the right. Climb the track on the right to arrive at the trig point on the summit of The Calf. From here take the path heading north-west and after about 300 yards when this path bends to the left continue on a grassy path straight ahead. Soon the path becomes more northerly before heading north-west again over Bush Howe.

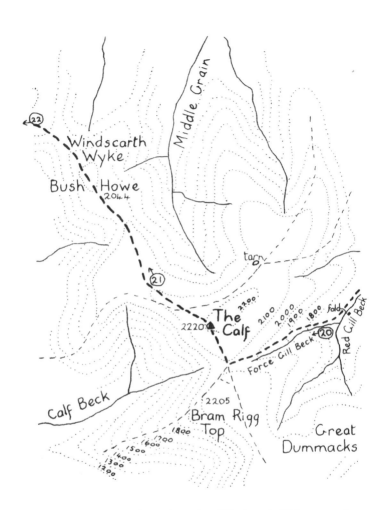

The path descends to the col at Windscarth Wyke, ascends to Breaks Head then curves round to the prominent cairn on Fell Head. Over to the north-west can be seen the Whinfell Ridge, fortunately now saved from having a forest of wind turbines on it, and beyond that the Lakeland fells.

Fell Head
2045

Breaks Head

Long Rigg

Long Rigg Beck

Whin's End

23

Beck Houses Gate

24

fold

gates

Beck House

View to Fell Head from Beck Houses Gate

Lowgill Viaduct

As the path descends towards Whin's End the turbines at Grayrigg and the striking arches of the disused viaduct at Lowgill come into view. Soon the path levels out and at a large clump of rushes follow the track round to the left: this track widens out and drops down around the head of Ellergill Beck. Soon, at an indistinct fork take a grass path on the right which gradually descends, in the direction of the wind farm, towards Beck House in the trees ahead. At a wall corner go through three gates then descend the meadow heading down towards the beck and the trees that surround Beck House. On approaching the trees a fence around the farm complex crosses the beck and to the right is a gate. Cross the beck, go through the gate and two further gates then, passing to the left of the farmhouse, take the farm drive to Howgill Lane.

Turn left but soon take the path on the right (FP via Riddings ¼m) and at a wall corner take the stile in a section of fencing. Continue, with the wall to the left, through another gate where a marker post points left to go through the farm buildings at

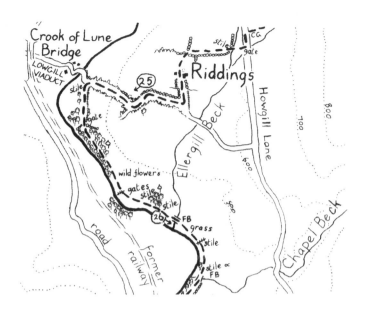

Riddings. The farm drive leads onto a minor road, here turn right and follow it for about ½ mile until, at a bend, the Crook of Lune Bridge comes into view.

This landmark bridge, which marked the county boundary between the West Riding of Yorkshire and Westmorland, is well worth a visit. Take a stile on the left (FP Thwaite 1¼m) to join the Dales Way and follow this waymarked path which stays close to the river through gates, over stiles and footbridges.

At a bridge (FP Dales Way) cross the beck and almost immediately enter the cobbled courtyard of Hole House with its lovely floral displays which at the time of writing were a riot of colour. Exit the farmyard through two gates straight ahead onto the fellside and turn right. Over the hill take the right of two facing gates and go straight ahead keeping the wall on the left. At the end of the wall ignore a wicket gate and take the path (FP Bramaskew) and almost

Crook of Lune Bridge

immediately another wicket gate on the left leads onto a farm track. This short track drops down to cross over a beck and two gates and then follows initially a hedge then a wall on the left. After weaving around a small barn the path heads up the hillside keeping left to a ladder stile in a short section of wall to the left of three mature trees. Just past another barn is a stile in the facing wall. Aim half right across the field where a gate to the left of a metal gate is taken which leads onto a footpath between a hedge on the left and a stone wall on the right. This leads into open meadowland and a large field is crossed with a short isolated stretch of stone wall in it: head towards a ladder stile to the left of a barn with another ladder stile in the facing wall ahead.

Between the two ladder stiles the route turns left on a track leading from Low Branthwaite, crosses the beck and immediately takes a stile on the right. Head up the bank towards a finger post and the direction of the route is the one 'indicated', at present, by

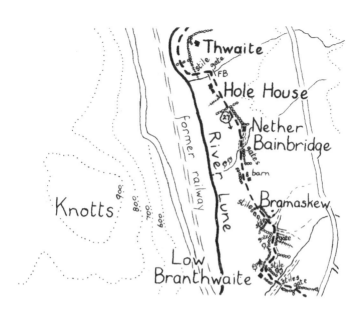

Low Branthwaite

the broken arm of the finger post. It is here that the Dales Way is left by taking the stile heading straight up the field to a wicket gate at the end of a stretch of wall on the right.

Through the gate head gently up the field to the left and continue heading up the meadow between a barn on the left and a farmhouse on the right to a wicket gate in the facing wall. Turn right on the lane and opposite the entrance drive to Ruecrofts a signpost (FP Underwinder ⅓m) indicates the way ahead through a wooden gate. Follow the wall on the left to a gate then head towards the right of the barn conversion at Ash-hining Farm.

The view from here is towards Middleton Fell which will be climbed on the next stage of the route. Go through a metal gate on the left and another metal gate on the right then half right across the field to locate a ladder stile in a short stretch of facing wall. Follow the wall on the right over the brow of the hill and drop down to a stile in a short piece of fence corner. Drop down through two gates to enter the complex of Underwinder. After passing the barn conversion, Greenmantle, on the left turn left through a gate with a FP sign. After going through the back garden take a stile into a meadow, following the hedgerow on the left through a wicket gate and then to a stile by a metal gate which leads onto a lane. This lane is followed right for about a mile into Sedbergh. On approaching the town a playing field and children's playground are passed, next to Sedbergh People's Hall, and are followed by three Victorian four-storied semi-detached houses on the right. The lane meets the A683: turn left and almost immediately on the right is St Andrew's Church and the end of this stage.

Note :-
Pennine Journey
route heads for
Dentdale and
Whernside

DAY FOUR

Sedburgh to Barbon

Distance	11¼ miles
Highest Point	1,985 feet
Height Ascended	2,217 feet
Going	Moderate with one long climb
Map	O.S. Explorer OL19 & OL2

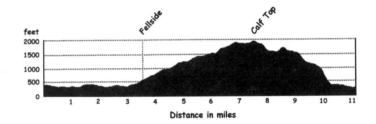

Sedbergh has developed its reputation immensely since, in *Walks on the Howgill Fells*, AW described it as 'the capital of the region'. He also said it was best known for Sedbergh School – 'the large Public School long established in its midst' – founded in 1525 by Roger Lupton who it is believed came from Cautley. However, since that guidebook was written this attractive market town of around 3,000 residents has become better known throughout the world as a Book Town – one of only three in the United Kingdom. Started as a venture to attract visitors following the severe problems caused by the 2001 Foot and Mouth epidemic it built rapidly on several book businesses already in the town and is now well established.

Sedbergh's economic importance and geographical location by the River Lune made it an essential station on the Ingleton–Tebay railway. It is also well known to long-distance footpath walkers as a staging post on the popular Dales Way, part of which was used to enter Sedbergh.

This section of the Trail is essentially a bridge between the Howgill Fells and the start of *Walks in Limestone Country* at Ingleton.

Sedbergh

After leaving St Andrew's Church it passes through the various buildings and playing fields of Sedbergh School before crossing the River Rawthey on a 40 yards long footbridge and then the River Dee just before its confluence with the Rawthey. After meeting the disused Ingleton–Tebay line again, the route comes close to the River Lune before it swings away to climb Middleton Fell. On this ascent can be seen views of the Howgill Fells before reaching the summit of the ridge at Calf Top (1,999 feet). A delightful ridge walk terminates at the cairn on Eskholme Pike on its rocky knoll overlooking Barbon with extensive views of the Lune valley and its approach to Morecambe Bay. From here a steep descent and a walk through part of the grounds of Barbon Manor soon lead to the War Memorial in the village centre.

Route Description

From the junction of Main Street and Finkle Street by St Andrew's Church head down Finkle Street with the church to the right and just after the War Memorial take a metalled path on the right which passes, on the left, the cricket ground of Sedbergh School. Take a path (FP Birks ½m) on the left continuing round the cricket ground which crosses a driveway between school buildings to a kissing gate and drops down to another kissing gate at a road. Cross the road and go another kissing gate onto a path (FP Birks ⅓m) which passes between some of the school's sports facilities. At another kissing gate (FP Birks) follow the track as it climbs gently around a house to arrive at a lane at another kissing gate. Turn left and pass, on the left, an interesting cottage which carries two date stones 218 years apart (1762 and 1980). Continue along the lane which bends to the left following the course of the River Rawthey and take, opposite the old mill at Birks, a footbridge on the left (FP Catholes ⅓m)

Abbot Holme Bridge

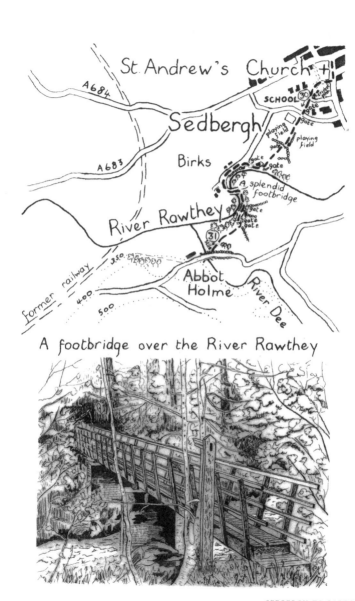

A footbridge over the River Rawthey

which has a span of around forty paces. Over the river the path climbs gently to the right and follows the river, through trees, to reach a gate (SP Abbot Holme Bridge). Cross the golf course and where the path splits bear half right through an opening into a field which is crossed, with a wall on the left, to reach a lane. Here turn right to cross the bridge over the River Dee just before it enters the Rawthey.

Continue on the lane, passing cottages on the right and climb to meet a T-junction. Turn right and soon a sign on the left (BW) points across the lower slopes of the hillside. Go to the right of the middle pylon to reach a gate in a facing wall. Take a green track close to a wall on the right which after another gate becomes enclosed between broken-down walls. The path meets a wall with a gate near by on the left which leads onto a lane. Turn left and follow the lane straight ahead (ignoring an underpass under a disused railway) for approximately ¾ mile to meet the A683 (Sedbergh to Kirkby Lonsdale road) to turn left and soon take a lane on the left (FP Fellside; Barbon).

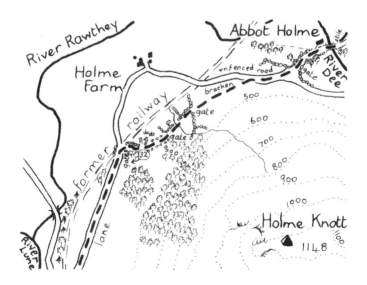

This lane winds gently uphill to a renovated farmhouse. Take the gate to the left of the farmhouse onto a stony track which continues to climb gently ahead. The track leads through the left hand of two facing gates and soon arrives at a beck. NB The following section may be difficult in low mist due to the terrain. Take the grassy, right hand path away from the beck, skirting the bracken, and not a stony track on the left. Head up the fellside and, ignoring the first minor path off to the right, take the second path on the right, keeping to this path and ignoring other minor quad bike tracks on the right. After crossing another beck look back to see the wind turbines at Grayrigg and a distant M6 – both in evidence on Day Three's walk – against the background of the Lakeland Fells. The path reaches another beck which provides the final opportunity to top up water containers, as the majority of the final 6 miles into Barbon is on the high escarpment overlooking Barbondale.

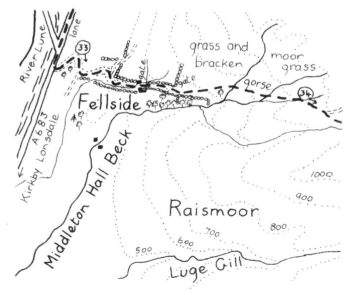

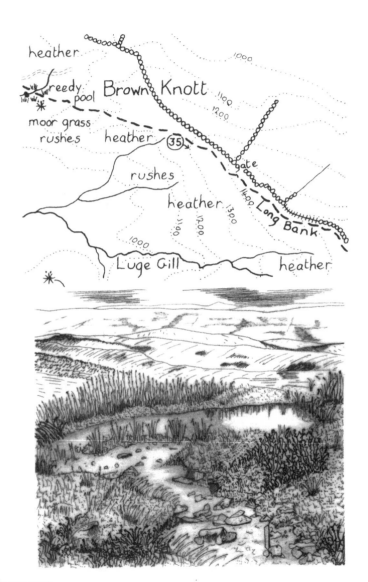

Dentdale

Soon, as the path rises, the summits of some of the Howgill Fells begin to immerge over the walled ridge of Holme Knott on the left. Shortly, a very large, flat, rectangular stone is reached, to the right of the path in a flatter, grassy area. Twenty yards further on take a faint path on the right which climbs away from the main path to reach, in a few yards, a small reedy pool from where the onward path is now clearly visible. (If this path is missed and the ridge wall is reached, on looking back the path will be clearly visible.) The path winds its way through the heather, seen at its best in August, to meet up with the stone wall along the ridge which is followed for around 3 miles. At a high point, where a short section of the wall has fallen away and been replaced by a wire fence, ahead is a lovely view of Dentdale with the village of Dent just peeping out behind the shoulder of the hillside.

Look back here for a lovely panorama of the Howgill Fells and Sedbergh between the Lune and Rawthey valleys. The path cuts a corner away from the wall, where two prominent cairns are visible on

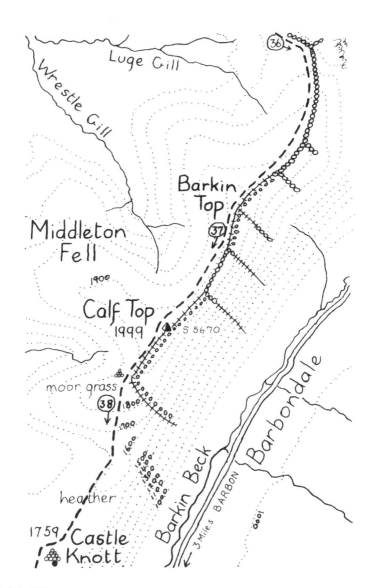

Luge Gill

Wrestle Gill

Middleton
Fell

Barkin
Top

③⑦

1900

Calf Top
1999

S 5670

moor grass

③⑧

1800

1700

1600

1500
1400
1300
1200
1100

heather

Barkin Beck

3 Miles BARBON

Barbondale

1759 Castle
Knott

1000

③⑥

the skyline ahead, and then rejoins the wall for the steady ascent to the high point of this stage at Calf Top with its trig point. On this climb can be had lovely views of upper Dentdale. The summit of Calf Top provides views in all directions, from a distant Blackpool Tower (seen by following the line of the wall stretching away from the trig point) round to the Howgill Fells with, to the east, the summit of Ingleborough. Soon after starting the descent, at a wall corner the path forsakes the wall and drops down towards a col then heads up towards the cairn on the top of Castle Knott. It continues on past another cairn and descends to a prominent cairn on Eskholme Pike on its rocky knoll. Below is Barbon with, near by, Kirkby Lonsdale and an extensive view of the Lune valley.

Drop down through boulders keeping to the left of a striking rock outcrop then head straight down towards the prominent trees which surround the farm of Eskholme to a gate in the facing wall.

Barbon from Eskholme Pike

The path then drops down to the farm where, at a gate, direction markers point left away from the property towards a gate in the boundary wall of the grounds of Barbon Manor. The path now stays close to a wood on the right and at the end of the trees a marker post points diagonally right across the meadow to an underpass in the old Ingleton–Tebay railway. Once through, keep to the higher ground heading towards the farmhouse on the right which is passed to reach a lane by the bridge over Barbon Beck. Turn left and at the T-junction turn left again to arrive at the War Memorial in the centre of Barbon close to the Barbon Inn.

A view to Bridge End, Barbon, as the path passes under the former Sedbergh to Ingleton railway.

DAY FIVE

Barbon to Ingleton

Distance	11 miles
Highest Point	1,010 feet
Height Ascended	1,715 feet
Going	Moderate
Map	O.S. Explorer OL2

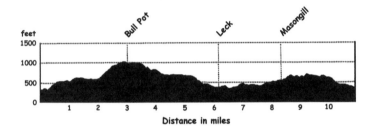

Barbon is a small village on the edge of Cumbria situated very close to where Cumbria, North Yorkshire and Lancashire meet. If current proposals for the extension of the Yorkshire Dales National Park are implemented then Barbon will come within the enlarged Park's boundary. The village nestles at the foot of Barbondale where Barbon Beck emerges from its wooded confines between the steep slopes of Thorn Moor and Barbon Low Fell before entering the River Lune.

Barbon is another community on this walk that was on the Ingleton-Tebay line with its own station situated behind the Barbon Inn. It was, though, on the more ancient route of a Roman road from Ribchester which linked up with the Maiden Way and then on to Kirkby Thore and Hadrian's Wall.

The manor of Barbon was held by Earl Tosti, who was killed in the Battle of Stamford Bridge fighting against King Harold, and is mentioned in the Domesday Book Survey. In 1591 the manor was bought by the Shuttleworth family and it is still in the ownership of the family today. The present Barbon Manor, built in the style of a French chateau in 1863, is well known as the venue of two major hillclimbs – for motor cars and motorcycles.

Barbon Manor

The trail undergoes a gradual transformation during this stage as the route enters limestone country. After a short walk up the drive of Barbon Manor using part of the hillclimb track the path follows Barbon Beck through its wooded valley within the manor's grounds to emerge onto the fellside.

A track winds around between Barbon High Fell and Barbon Low Fell to arrive at Bullpot Farm, the base of the Red Rose Cave and Pothole Club. Very soon, and right by the path, is Bull Pot of the Witches, from which the farmhouse gets its name: approach with extreme caution. The OS Explorer map for the area shows the high number of potholes in the vicinity and the route threads its way

Ireby

between them to arrive at the surprising and impressive Kirk Gill. Here the county of Lancashire is entered briefly while crossing a finger of land enclosing Leck Fell, Leck and the neighbouring hamlet of Ireby. In Leck the trail passes Leck Hall, the present home of Lord Shuttleworth, Lord Lieutenant of Lancashire.

From Ireby the path is essentially pastoral as it makes its way through farmland to the hamlet of Masongill. Here the attractive Masongill House, built around 1750, is passed as more farmland is crossed to reach Ingleton where the dominating arches of the railway viaduct make a surprising appearance as the town is entered.

Route Description

From the War Memorial continue along the road and turn left along the lane past St Bartholomew's Church. This crosses Barbon Beck, continues straight ahead and after a bend a marker post indicates a path (BW) on the right. This grassy path leads to a gate then becomes a broad track which continues through woodland above Barbon Beck for approximately 1¼ miles.

After a gate the path goes through some old oak trees, as it opens out at the end of the woods, to cross a concrete footbridge onto the road and turn right. The area around the bridge in the summer is a picnicker's paradise. Follow the road over a bridge and take a track leading off on the left (BW Bullpot 1m). The track winds its way through the bracken onto the open fell side, and where it begins to level out over to the left what appears to be the remains of an old limestone quarry can be seen. At a gate the path becomes a wide, walled track and where this meets a metalled road turn left (FP Easegill Kirk). The road ceases almost immediately, and by Bullpot Farm (now the base of the Red Rose Cave and Pothole Club) a marker post (FP to Ease Gill via Hellot Scales) points to the left of the buildings through a kissing gate with a plaque in memory of Mark Woodhouse, 1980. This initially stony track keeps to the left hand side of a wall

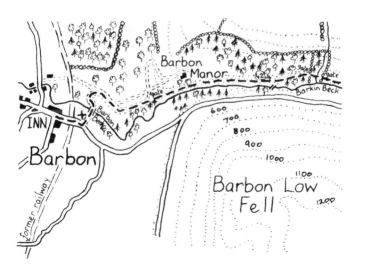

Barbon

Barbon Brook

and soon passes Bull Pot of the Witches in a clump of trees on the right with the smaller pothole of Hidden Pot on the left just before the path climbs in front of a double limekiln.

With the wall always to the right and a line of shake holes on the left continue along the grassy path and over a stile by a gate. Cow Pot, Lancaster Hole and the Ease Gill System are over to the left but the route continues straight on for about ¾ mile to arrive, surprisingly, at the edge of a deep, dry valley – Ease Gill. Take a sheep track to drop down to a ladder stile in a wall corner below and follow the gully for about 150 yards. The path crosses over to the left hand side of the beck opposite two ash trees in a section of fencing on the right. A small cairn marks the spot and from here the path climbs on a faint track bending right beneath four hawthorn trees in a limestone

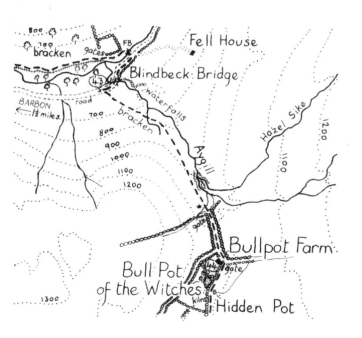

Bullpot Farm

outcrop to skirt around a rocky gully. This is a very dramatic section but requires some care, especially in wet conditions. In summer the path is not obvious as it goes through high bracken but soon broadens out and becomes obvious as it contours the hillside above Leck Beck for about ¾ mile before passing to the left of a ruined building by a large sycamore tree. (The public footpath heads directly across the fellside but there is a faint track that stays closer to the beck to eventually reach the footpath.)

Take a ladder stile over a wall and after crossing a small beck the path heads towards the intake wall. The path stays close to the fence and when it drops down to cross a beck ignore the path over the stile on the right and keep to the main path which climbs ahead. The path heads towards a plantation and arrives at a gate by an 'Open Access'

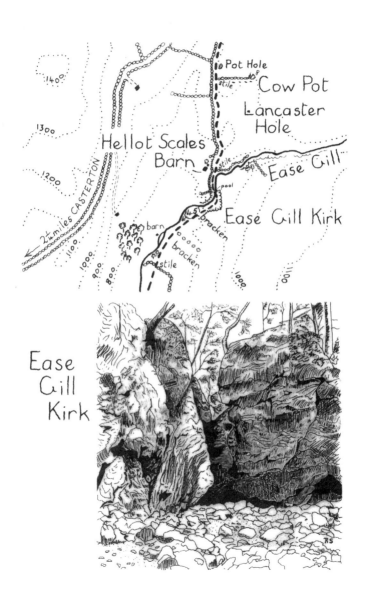

Pot Hole

stile

Cow Pot

Lancaster
Hole

1400

1300

Hellot Scales
Barn

Ease Gill

1200

stile

pool

2¾ miles CASTERTON

Ease Gill Kirk

1100

45

bracken

barn

1000

bracken

900

800

stile

1000

1000

1100

Ease
Gill
Kirk

RS

map. Do not take the gate but with the wall to the right follow it to cross a series of ladder stiles. After the third stile when the wall on the right bends away to the right to another corner, head straight across the meadow to a gate. Drop down the meadow but stay close to the wall and take another ladder stile on the right. A grassy path soon becomes a track and arrives at the first buildings of Leck by a ladder stile and gate. Take the tarmac lane through the village, turn left at a fork and at a crossroads head straight on to reach Leck primary school. Waymark signs point the way to the right of the buildings, through a gate then around the play area and pass through the car park of St Peter's Church onto a lane.

Leck School for Girls

Turn left and follow the lane which, after passing the old school, skirts around Leck Hall, for about ¾ mile past a farm and its buildings and where the lane bends right locate a sign at a gate on the left (Public Footpath) which points to a ladder stile in a facing wall.

High Park

Anneside
(ruins)

Springs Wood

moor grass

46

moor grass
Open Access Notice
stile   rushes
stile   grass

stile
Castle Hill

Leck Beck

stile

47
gate
stile

Leck

stile
SCHOOL
JUBILEE
COTTAGE

Lodge Farm

A65

road

48

Todgill Farm

In Leck, JUBILEE
COTTAGE, 1977, has the
following inscription :–
This SCHOOL for GIRLS was
erected by the surviving sisters
of R.H. WELCH Esq. in memory
of him and in aid of his
Designs for the Improvement
of Education.
1847

Keep to the wall and then a fence on the left to take a gate in the top corner of the field. With the wall now on the right for a few yards, drop down to a stile and onto a road. Turn right into the village of Ireby.

Just past the telephone kiosk, cross the beck and immediately turn right down a track which bends left and ceases at a gate by a barn. Take a stile to the left of the gate and climb gently up the hill on a grassy track to a wall corner. From here, with Ingleborough in the distance, follow the wall on the left for a short distance to enter a large meadow with Masongill ahead. Take a stile in the facing wall then cross the field to a stile in a wall corner which is reached by a wooden footbridge. The path then heads up the right hand edge of the next field. On approaching a wall corner, where the hedgerow ceases, look out for a stile at the start of the wall on the right which may be hidden by the hedge. At the wall corner aim slightly right to a facing gate and from there head half right up the meadow to a stile at the right hand corner of a boundary wall of a cottage. The path goes through the cottage garden to meet a lane in the hamlet of Masongill. Turn right along the lane which bends left to meet another road. Turn left and after about 100 yards take a stile on the right (FP Westgate 1¼m). Although the route heads for Westgate the sign points in the wrong direction, so head left walking in front of Masongill House and the nearby trees to gently ascend the meadow. On cresting the rise the outlying barns of Masongill Hall can be seen. Head for these and in the field corner by a barn is a kissing gate by a metal gate which leads onto the farm drive. Cross to a ladder stile which at the time of writing had broken steps: these can be avoided by going round the corner of the wall and through a metal gate. As the concrete track bends right climb the meadow ahead with a hedgerow to the left. After a while, head slightly right away from the hedge to a stile in the wall corner.

Once over the stile keep to the right of the wall and head to the farm at Fell Side. Go over another stile in the wall corner and head for the farm buildings. A series of gates leads around the barns and

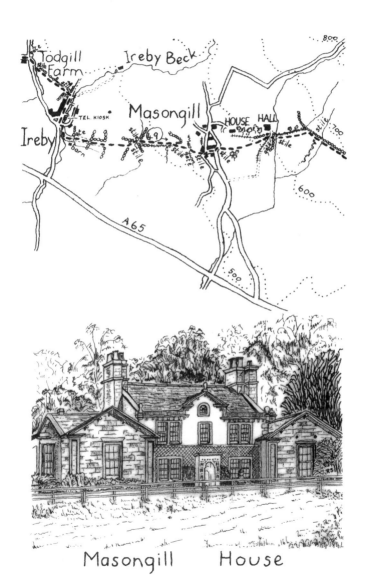

Masongill House

farmhouse and before the final gate leads onto the open meadow there is a huge sycamore tree. A grassy track by the wall heads down and crosses a delightful little valley before rising up again through a gate to another stile in the wall corner. Just before reaching the ladder stile there are some unlikely paving stones which cross a damp area. From a stile through a facing hedge the next objective on this section, the farm of Westgate, can be seen ahead and on the left the unmistakable shape of Ingleborough. Keep by the wall to a stile and wicket gate in the left hand corner of the field to the left of the farm buildings. Once over turn right towards a gate and stile with a wicket gate onto a lane. On the other side of the lane take the stile and wicket gate (West View ¾m) and with the wall to the left go straight ahead to another of the substantial stone stiles with wicket gates around this farm. Here the path goes by a small, new plantation. Cross a little beck to another stile in a wall corner and head on to yet another stile. The ruins of Cowgill farm are ahead and after passing between the buildings take a ladder stile by a gate. From here head straight across to another stile and wicket by a gate and keep to the right of the wall until buildings come into view on the right. Head towards them and locate a gate between a large house and a derelict barn. A short stretch of over-grown track leads onto a metalled road where the route turns right. At the wide entrance to Thornton Hall turn left (FP Ingleton ¾m) but at the next gate turn right off the drive down to a stile in a wall corner by a barn. Head straight down the field to a gate in the facing wall and take a stile to its left. Continue on to a direction marker at a wall corner by the nearer of two barns then follow the wall on the left to a kissing gate where a wire fence across the meadow meets the wall. Through the gate continue on by the wall to another kissing gate in the wall corner. Through the trees ahead can be seen Ingleton Viaduct, once used by two competing railway companies with stations at either end. The track drops down to the road by the start of the Ingleton Waterfalls Walk – a convenient place to end this stage.

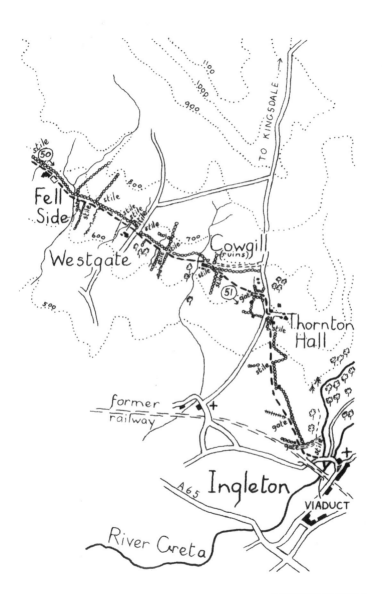

DAY SIX

Ingleton to Horton in Ribblesdale

Distance	12½ miles
Highest Point	2,372 feet
Height Ascended	2,777 feet
Going	Strenuous with one steep climb
Map	O.S. Explorer OL2

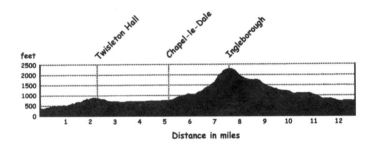

Ingleton advertises itself as being at 'the heart of the Three Peaks country'. It is certainly at the centre of this potholing and caving territory and so is extremely well situated for visitors, particularly walkers. But its seemingly tranquil setting and ambience belies its past. In addition to the quarrying that is still evident, it seems hard to accept that coal mining was a staple industry here with the only remnant being New Village – built for the miners and their families. Cotton mills, powered by water mills, were in abundance. There is also a very famous, and intriguing, literary connection. Sir Arthur Conan Doyle's mother lived at Masongill, through which the trail passes on its way to Ingleton, and he was married at St Oswald's Church in nearby Thornton in Lonsdale. At this time the vicar of Ingleton was the Reverend Todd Sherlock and as the area below the splendid viaduct by the church is called the Holmes, need one say more?

Ingleton Viaduct

Ingleborough, which in *Walks in Limestone Country* AW mentions as 'probably the most ascended mountain in the country outside Lakeland', dominates the town. Its summit, which the trail visits during this stage, is a broad plateau on which there is a 15-acre Iron Age hill fort. A recent archaeological survey found traces of a small seventh-century partly stone-built building and flint tools from the Early Neolithic period.

One of the famous attractions of Ingleton is the Falls Walk and this stage uses the initial climb up the falls, passing Thornton Force to meet, near Twisleton Hall, the Pennine Journey route where it comes down from Whernside on its way into Ingleton. At this point two alternative routes are offered. The main route continues along the minor road up the valley to Chapel-le-Dale, where it passes the delightfully situated St Leonard's Church. This late-seventeenth-century church contains a memorial dedicated to the workers who perished during the building of the Settle–Carlisle

Thornton Force

railway and the viaduct at Ribblehead which is visible from the ascent of Ingleborough.

The alternative, for those who within the Trail wish to ascend the Three Peaks, ascends the Pennine Journey route in reverse to the summit of Whernside and then crosses the valley to meet the main route on its ascent of Ingleborough. From the summit the trail heads to Horton in Ribblesdale passing through a magnificent limestone pavement with improving views of Penyghent, which overlooks the village.

Route Description

The Waterfalls Walk is on private land and involves an entrance charge which is well worth the expense as it has stunning views of some of the finest falls in Northern England. The walk is open at 9 a.m. every day of the year apart from Christmas Day. Pass the café and toilets on the left, buy a ticket at the entrance booth and

*Pecca Twin Falls

53

700

600

500

Swilla Glen

River Twiss

Pennine Journey route

River Doe

CHAPEL-LE-DALE

2½ miles →

52

+ Ingleton

B6255

1000

900

800

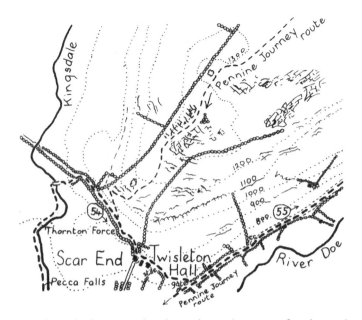

pass through the car park. The path winds its way for almost 2 miles through the ancient woodlands of Swilla Glen by the River Twiss and passes Pecca Falls and Thornton Force to emerge at the top of the falls in wonderful limestone countryside.

Cross the bridge over the Twiss and climb the zigzag steps and then a field to reach a track. After turning right there are two alternatives. *For those wishing to take in the Three Peaks on their Trail, using an OS map, take a path on the left which uses the Pennine Journey route in reverse to reach Bruntscar. From here take the obvious Three Peaks Walk path for the ascent of Whernside and return to Bruntscar before crossing the valley to Southerscales Nature Reserve – see map on page 87.* The main route continues past Twisleton Hall before dropping down the field to reach a lane. Turn left and follow this quiet lane along the valley of the River Doe for approximately 2½ miles between the impressive Twisleton Scar on the left and Raven Scar on the right. Over

St Leonard's Church,
Chapel-le-Dale

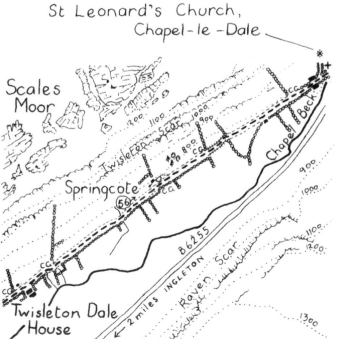

to the right the entrance to the popular White Scar Caves can be seen. The quiet hamlet of Chapel-le-Dale is reached with its church dedicated to St Leonard and soon the B6255.

Cross over, take the stile (FP Ingleborough 2m) and head straight across the field to a stile with a wicket gate in the facing wall. The path winds up to the right to another gate to pass in front of the farm buildings, and then continues on through a gateway and a gate to the right of a derelict barn to enter Southerscales Nature Reserve. Keep close to the left hand wall to climb towards a ladder stile but before reaching the stile the path doubles back to the right. This grassy path reaches a stony track – the route of the popular Three Peaks Walk. It is here that the alternative route joins the main route. Turn right towards Ingleborough, pass Braithwaite Wife Hole and soon arrive at a gate in a facing wall – soon after the gate look back for a good view of Whernside and the Ribblehead Viaduct.

Whernside

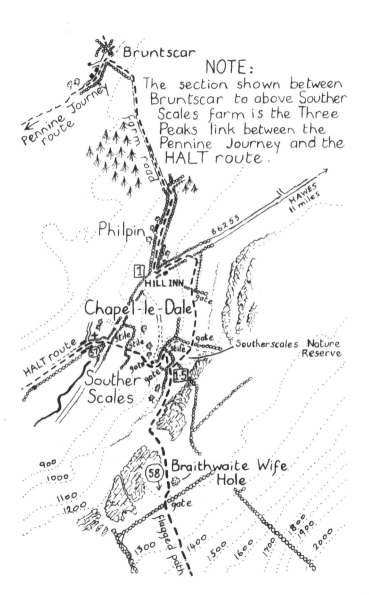

Bruntscar

NOTE:
The section shown between Bruntscar to above Souther Scales farm is the Three Peaks link between the Pennine Journey and the HALT route.

Pennine Journey route

road

HAWES 11 miles

B6255

Philpin

1

HILL INN

gate

Chapel-le-Dale

HALT route

stile

stile

gate

stile

gate

Southerscales Nature Reserve

57

gate

15

Souther Scales

gate

900
1000
1100
1200

58

Braithwaite Wife Hole

gate

flagged path

1300   1400   1500   1600   1700   1800   1900   2000

The path is essentially man-made with large 'flags', boardwalks over damp areas and flagged steps. Eventually the path becomes steeply pitched as it climbs the facing escarpment to reach a kissing gate. From now on the gradient eases and the path soon reaches the summit plateau. Keep to the right hand edge (but not too close) to arrive at a cross-walled wind shelter with its view indicator close to the summit cairn.

Ingleborough

Return along the, now, left hand side of the plateau, take the path previously ascended but very soon at a fork turn right and follow a clear track heading for the distant Penyghent. The path crosses a double ladder stile and after passing a ruined building crosses a beck to reach another gate (FP Horton in R 2¾).

At a fork keep left towards the wall on the left and Penyghent (if visible), to pass through some wonderful limestone pavements within Ingleborough National Nature Reserve. Two successive finger posts point the way ahead. Horton in Ribblesdale soon comes into

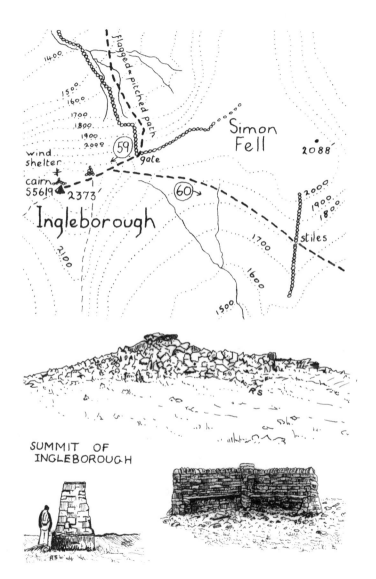

SUMMIT OF
INGLEBOROUGH

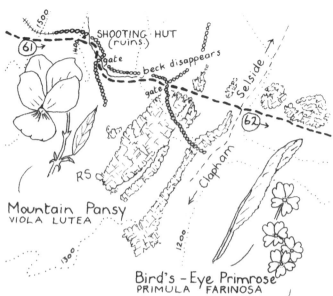

61→

1500

1400

SHOOTING HUT (ruins)

gate

beck disappears

gate

Selside

62→

Clapham

RS

1200

1300

Mountain Pansy
VIOLA LUTEA

Bird's-Eye Primrose
PRIMULA FARINOSA

Flowers of the limestone

The remains of
the old shooting hut

The path through the limestone pavement

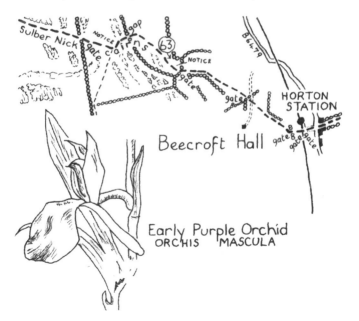

Beecroft Hall

Early Purple Orchid
ORCHIS MASCULA

A flower of the limestone

St Oswald's Church, Horton in Ribblesdale

view dominated by the bulk of Penyghent, and after crossing the farm drive to Beecroft Hall the path soon arrives at Horton station. Cross the line and head down the station approach road to reach the B6479 and turn right to soon cross the footbridge over the River Ribble into the Yorkshire Dales NPA car park with its toilets. Walk through the village, pass St Oswald's church and on to the green where a Millennium Stone placed there by Horton Flower Club ends this stage.

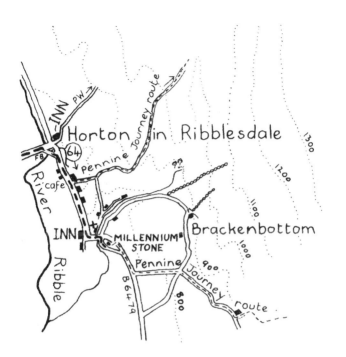

DAY SEVEN

Horton in Ribblesdale to Settle

Distance	12 miles
Highest Point	2,267 feet
Height Ascended	2,744 feet
Going	Strenuous with one steep climb
Map	O.S. Explorer OL2

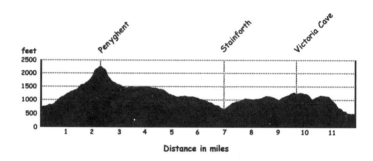

For long-distance footpath walkers, Horton in Ribblesdale marks the junction of the Pennine Way, the Ribble Way, the Pennine Journey and now the Howgills and Limestone Trail. However, for endurance walkers it is the traditional start and finish of one of the most famous ones – the 24-mile Three Peaks Walk over the summits of Whernside, Ingleborough and Penyghent. Horton in Ribblesdale is one of the leading centres in Great Britain for caving and pot holing with, north of the village, Alum Pot and the Long Churn cave system and, on the western side of Penyghent, Hunt Pot and Hull Pot. The Trail does not pass Hull Pot which, at 300 feet in length and 60 feet in width and depth, is the largest hole in the country. Those walkers who do wish to see this remarkable geological feature can do so, using their O.S. map, by taking the

Penyghent

Pennine Way to it before retracing their steps briefly and ascending Penyghent to meet the main route at its summit.

The main route leaves the Millennium Stone on the green and ascends Penyghent via Brackenbottom. After passing the immense shakehole, Churn Milk Hole, the trail meets, on reaching Moor Head Lane, the outward route of the Pennine Journey as it makes its way from Stainforth. The trail takes an alternative route into the village and, after using stepping stones to cross Stainforth Beck, makes its way to Catrigg Force. This is a gem of a waterfall set in a deep secluded gorge and AW describes it in *Walks in Limestone Country* as 'a double waterfall of 60 feet in a very lovely setting'. Its situation made it, reputedly, the composer Elgar's favourite place in the area. The trail then makes its way through some dramatic limestone land-scape passing Victoria Cave below Attermire Scar before arriving in Settle. The Trail ends at Settle station from where AW set out on 25 September 1938 on his Pennine Journey. A blue plaque in an information room on the platform commemorates this notable event.

Do not rush away from Settle, one of the most delightful market towns of the Yorkshire Dales. It will repay the time spent in exploring its narrow streets and shady corners on an interesting Town Trail. It is seen at its best on a sunny market day (Tuesday) when the market square which fronts the busy A65 road is crammed with stalls and the two-storey Shambles provides an attractive focal point. Settle, although just outside the boundary of the Yorkshire Dales National Park, is an ideal centre for walkers of all ages and capabilities – 'a gateway to the hills'. However, if a change is needed then the return train journey to/from Carlisle offers a delightful, scenic trip through the beautiful countryside of the Ribble valley, over the magnificent Ribblehead Viaduct and through the Eden valley to the historic city of Carlisle – the major Roman settlement on Hadrian's Wall which was the primary objective of AW when he set out from Settle on his Pennine Journey.

Route Description

From the Millennium Stone head towards the church and take the lane to the right of the beck which passes the village primary school. This pleasant lane passes initially through woodland, then fields and just before the first building in Brackenbottom take a footpath on the left (FP Penyghent Summit 1¾m).

After a gate the path heads upwards with the wall on the left and soon Penyghent comes into view. The path is clear ahead and after a stretch of large 'paving' stones eventually arrives at a gate to join the Pennine Way. Turn left for the final climb to the summit

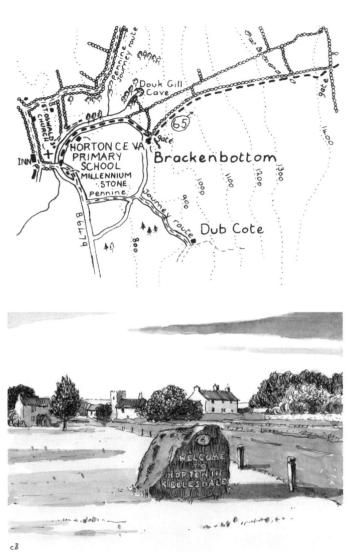

Millennium Stone

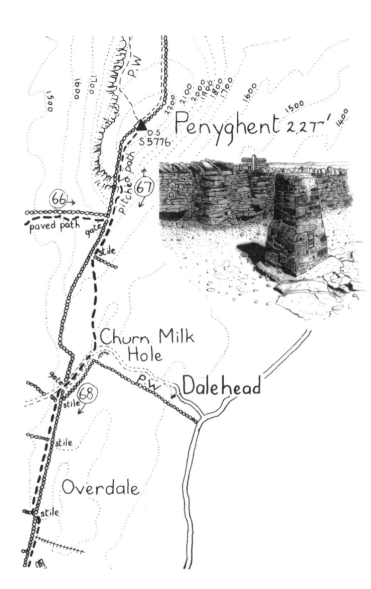

P.W

1500 · 1600 · 1700

P.W

△ O.S S5776

Penyghent 2,277′

2200 · 2100 · 2000 · 1900 · 1700 · 1600 · 1500 · 1400

66 →

Pitched path

67 ↓

paved path

gate

stile

Churn Milk Hole

P.W

Dalehead

gate

68 ↓

stile

stile

Overdale

stile

which incorporates stretches of pitched path to take the weight of the pedestrian traffic. In addition to the panoramic views from the summit of Penyghent there is also a splendid shelter incorporating seats built to commemorate the 50th Anniversary of the Yorkshire Dales National Park 12 October 2004. Return to the gate where the ascent met the Pennine Way and carry straight on. The path continues for about ½ mile to reach a track at a finger post close to Churn Milk Hole and turns right (Helwith Bridge).

Churn Milk Hole

On cresting a rise a finger post can be seen (Public Footpath) pointing the way half left towards a stile and wicket gate in the facing wall. Keeping the wall on the left continue ahead over wet terrain to another stile and wicket gate beyond which the ground is slightly drier. At a wall corner take a ladder stile adjacent to which are two finger posts. One points back to Churn Milk Hole and the other (Public Footpath) points the way ahead with the wall now on the right.

After the next ladder stile the path soon starts to descend gently before turning away from the wall to meet Moor Head Lane. Here the path meets the Pennine Journey route coming up from Stainforth. Turn left down Moor Head Lane and on meeting Goat Lane turn right and follow this quiet lane for about a mile into Stainforth. Take the stepping stones across Stainforth Beck, keep to the left of the village green and continue straight ahead on Goat Scar Lane (Pennine Bridleway). This stony track is taken for ¾ mile to arrive at three gates. Take the wicket gate on the left (SP Catrigg Foss Only) to visit the impressive Catrigg Force described in *Walks in Limestone Country* as 'a double waterfall of 60 feet in a very lovely setting'.

Return to the wicket gate; take the right hand gate and the obvious track ahead which rises to cross through a gate in the wall. Immediately take a path on the right (Pennine Bridleway Winskill ½) crossing the meadow which leads onto a track heading for Upper Winskill and High Winskill. At a junction of paths by the gates and cattle grids a finger post points the way left (Pennine Bridleway; Settle) along a metalled lane. At a T-junction, on meeting the road,

Catrigg Force

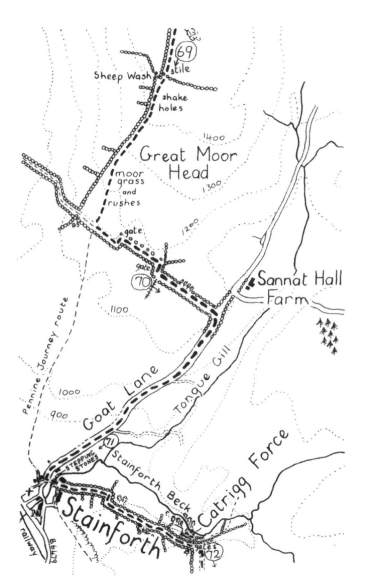

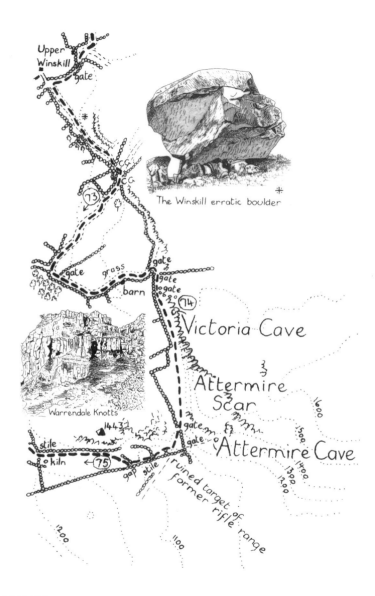

Upper
Winskill

gate

*

CG
CG

73

gate   grass   gate
              gate
barn   gate

74

Victoria Cave

Attermire
Scar

1600

1500

1400

1300

1200

1443

gate

gate

Attermire Cave

stile

kiln   75

gap stile

ruined target of
former rifle range

1200

1100

The Winskill erratic boulder

Warrendale Knotts

turn right (Pennine Bridleway; Settle 2) and follow the road to a sharp right hand bend. Take the stony track on the left (Public Byway Langscar Gate 4; Pennine Bridleway Settle Loop) following signs for the Victoria Cave and at a gate double back to the right (FP Victoria Cave). The path hugs the wall on the right and the large entrance to the Victoria Cave is just out of sight up to the left amid the limestone outcrops. **A warning notice strongly advises against exploring the cave.** Continue on the path and at a wall corner go straight ahead, with Attermire Scar up on the left, to reach a gate in a wall on the right. The path bends round through the grass to the right below the limestone outcrops to reach a finger post. Do not

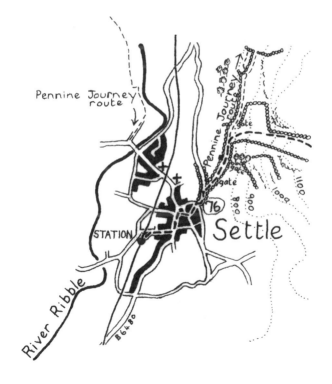

cross the stile but take the path (FP Banks Lane Settle 1m) keeping the wall to the left. From the finger post look up to the right to view the magnificent limestone outcrops. After a stile the path climbs gently and when meeting a section of wall on the right head right and follow a grassy path that skirts below the limestone crags of Warrendale Knotts.

Once through a wicket gate by a dilapidated metal gate the path descends with the Ribble valley ahead and Settle coming into view almost immediately. The path arrives at Banks Lane to meet at a finger post the Pennine Journey route; turn left towards Settle and at a ruined barn the path becomes stony and walled. Drop down the path following the Pennine Bridleway signs to take a narrow cobbled lane which reaches High Street. Cross to Cheapside passing the Town Hall on the right, turn left at the main road and then right into Station Road. Take the station approach to Settle station and the end of the walk.

Settle Station

POSTSCRIPT

Two differing themes came to the fore while we were doing the preliminary work on deciding the route of the Trail and then test walking it – railways and the Quaker movement. But it was only afterwards when we looked further into them that it became apparent how close the relationship between the two was.

The more dominant theme though was that of the railways, particularly the remains of the old railway network that was a major factor in the industrial revolution and brought so much prosperity to different parts of Britain. Within a mile of the start the route passes over the trackbed of the disused South Durham & Lancashire Union railway line (between Barnard Castle and Tebay) with Kirkby Stephen East station being bypassed 2 miles later. Just after mile 5, the site of the former Smardale station, now an attractively restored private house, on the same line is passed before the route joins the trackbed again to walk over the magnificent Smardalegill Viaduct.

On the opening stretch of the stage to Cautley there is the traffic noise of the nearby busy A685 but just over 40 years ago the noise would have been that of railway engines as the road is on what was the trackbed of the South Durham & Lancashire Union railway line mentioned earlier. Later in the stage can be seen the striking brick viaduct at Lowgill, one of three magnificent listed viaducts on this line – River Rawthey, Waterside and Lowgill.

It was just past Lowgill that the Ingleton branch of the North Western railway which went via Kirkby Lonsdale, Barbon, Middleton-on-Lune, and Sedbergh joined what is now the West Coast main line at Tebay.

These grand structures, which can be reached easily from the Trail, still dominate their landscapes and survive as memorials to a main line that never materialised. The line is then seen again when the Ingleton

Waterside Viaduct

viaduct comes into view as the Trail drops down into the village. This magnificent viaduct, with its 11 arches and a span of 800 feet, crosses the Swilla Glen. Ingleton epitomised the intense rivalry at the onset of railway building as the London & North Western Railway and Midland Railway opened stations at opposite ends of the valley where their lines terminated with all the consequent upheaval for passengers having to change trains. The viaduct was only built in 1859.

It is not until the Trail reaches Horton in Ribblesdale that the next historic line is crossed: that of the Settle–Carlisle line. The renowned Ribblehead Viaduct can be seen in the distance as the Trail makes its ascent from Chapel-le-Dale where, in the church of St Leonard, is a monument to all those who lost their lives during the building of the viaduct and the Settle–Carlisle railway. The trail ends at Settle station from where the 247 mile long Pennine Journey starts its circular route back to Settle.

The links between the Quaker movement and the early railway industry are unequivocal and well documented. In some respects the

Pulpit Rock

Trail provides a link between the two for it was on Firbank Fell, on the west side of the Lune valley through which the Trail passes, that George Fox preached a sermon on 13 June 1652 to a gathering of around 1,000 people having previously had a vision on Pendle Hill (scene of AW's earliest countryside expeditions from nearby Blackburn). It is commonly accepted that this sermon led to the formation of the Quaker movement or the Society of Friends. Firbank Fell lies between Kendal and Sedbergh and in an exhibition at the Friends Meeting House in Kendal there is a wonderful modern tapestry comprising panels made by Quakers from around the world. This depicts the influence of Quakers on the development of the modern world. In their ranks were pioneers of industry, commerce, science and medicine discoveries as well as leaders in the anti-slavery movement and social reform.

As regards the railway industry the so-called 'father of the railway', Edward Pease, was responsive to the ideas of George Stephenson which lead to the building of the first steam railway – the Stockton & Darlington railway. Other Quaker railway pioneers were Thomas

Bradshaw who achieved considerable renown for his comprehensive railway guides and Thomas Edmondson, a station master on the Newcastle & Carlisle Line, who developed the railway ticket.

The Society of Friends worship in Meeting Houses and the most well known one is at Brigflatts near Sedbergh, close to the Trail. Here, in June 1652, George Fox met some Westmorland Seekers before preaching in the churchyard of St Andrews Church in Sedbergh and later addressing the crowds on Firbank Fell. He established a Meeting at Brigflatts that year and in 1675 the present Meeting House was built.

Around that time the Meeting House at Settle, at the end of the Trail was built and it was at this building that the faith of a remarkable Settle family was established – the Birkbecks. George Birkbeck (1776–1841) founded the Mechanics' Institutes and John Birkbeck Senior founded the Craven Bank and was also a noted mountaineer and cave explorer. His son, also John, followed in his father's footsteps in banking and mountaineering.

Friends Meeting House, Settle

HOWGILLS AND LIMESTONE TRAIL,
AND THE AREA'S ASSOCIATED RAILWAYS.

SMARDALE VIADUCT
SMARDALE GILL VIADUCT
Kirkby Stephen
Tebay
Ravenstonedale
MAIN WEST COAST LINE
Wild Boar Fell
LOWGILL VIADUCT
The Calf
Cross Keys Cautley
Fox's Pulpit
WATERSIDE VIADUCT
Sedbergh
Garsdale Head
Brigflatts
RAWTHEY VIADUCT
Rawthey
Hawes
Ure
Eden
CARLISLE TO
Dent
Dee
ARTEN GILL VIADUCT
DENT HEAD VIADUCT
Barbon
Lune
Whernside
SETTLE TO
RIBBLEHEAD VIADUCT
Kirkby Lonsdale
Chapel le Dale
Penyghent
INGLETON VIADUCT
Ingleborough
Ingleton
Greta
Horton-in-Ribblesdale
CARNFORTH LINE
Clapham
Ribble
2·6 MILES
Stainforth
CLAPHAM STATION
Settle

BS

DISMANTLED RAILWAYS
A: NER: KIRKBY STEPHEN – PENRITH
B: NER: TEBAY – DARLINGTON
C: LNWR: LOWGILL – INGLETON
D: MR: INGLETON – CLAPHAM
E: MR: GARSDALE – HAWES
F: NER: HAWES – NORTHALLERTON

NOTE: HERITAGE RAILWAYS
A: EDEN VALLEY RAILWAY —WARCOP
E/F: WENSLEYDALE RAILWAY REDMIRE – LEEMING BAR.

READER'S LOG OF THE JOURNEY

Date	Section	N.G.R.
	Kirkby Stephen	NY 775 085
	Poetry Path	NY 777 080
	Waitby	NY 750 082
	Smardale Bridge	NY 720 059
	Ravenstonedale	NY 723 040
	Weasdale	NY 690 039
	Bowderdale	NY 677 046
	Bowderdale Head	SD 681 979
	Cautley (Cross Keys Inn)	SD 697 968
	The Calf	SD 667 970
	Whins End	SD 639 976
	Crook of Lune Bridge	SD 620 963
	Sedbergh (St Andrew's Church)	SD 657 921
	Fellside	SD 636 889
	Calf Top	SD 664 856
	Barbon	SD 628 825
	Bull Pot	SD 662 813
	Leck	SD 644 769
	Masongill	SD 664 752
	Ingleton	SD 693 732
	Twisleton Hall	SD 701 751
	Chapel-le-Dale	SD 737 771
	Ingleborough	SD 741 745
	Horton in Ribblesdale	SD 811 720
	Penyghent	SD 838 733
	Stainforth	SD 821 674
	Victoria Cave	SD 838 650
	Settle Station	SD 817 634

Miles		Times		Weather	
S	C	A	D		
-	-				
½	½				
4¼	4¼				
7¼	7¼				
8½	8½				
2½	11				
3½	12				
8	16½				
9½	18				
2½	20½				
5¼	23¼				
7¼	25¼				
11¾	29¾				
3¾	33½				
7½	37¼				
11¼	41				
3	44				
6¼	47¼				
8½	49½				
11	52				
2¼	54¼				
5¼	57¼				
7½	59½				
12½	64½				
2¼	66¾				
7	71½				
9¾	74¼				
12	76½				

INDEX TO PLACE-NAMES

Numbers in *italics* relate to place-names on the maps.